MW01036133

Anger,
Anxiety
and
Fear

A Biblical Perspective

Stuart Scott

Anger, Anxiety and Fear

©2009 by Stuart Scott

Excerpted from
THE EXEMPLARY HUSBAND
A Biblical Perspective
©2000 by Stuart Scott

Published by FOCUS PUBLISHING, Inc.
All Rights Reserved

No part of this book may be reproduced by any means
without written consent of the publisher
except for brief quotes used in reviews written specifically
for use in a magazine or newspaper.

Focus Publishing, Inc.
Post Office Box 665
Bemidji, MN   56619

Unless otherwise noted, all Scripture is taken from
The New American Standard Bible
©1960, 1962, 1963, 1971, 1973, 1975, 1977, 1995
by The Lockman Foundation
Used by permission

ISBN 1 885904-76-2

Printed in the United States of America

CONTENTS

Anger, Anxiety and Fear

ANGER

Our responsibility as Christians is to depend on God as we work toward becoming more like Him every day. Sometimes, there is a life-dominating sin that will greatly hinder a Christian from becoming more like Christ. In this booklet, I want to offer some biblical help for three such sins. In marriage counseling over the years, I have seen these problems again and again in the lives of husbands and wives. Even if we say we do not have a serious problem in these areas, we all have had experience with them and give way to them from time to time. We need to be on guard against these sins and know how to deal with temptation when it comes. We need to pray for God's help and avoid them as the detrimental sins they are. Obviously, before we can do this we must have a truly changed heart (salvation) and we must understand how in the world we can practically change.

For each one of these sins we need a clear *definition*, an *explanation*, a method of *examination*, and a path of *transformation*.

Sinful Anger Displeases God

Some people consider themselves possessed by the "anger demon" and think they are victims of an anger attack. They themselves feel as if their anger is something they cannot control. Some people talk about years of turmoil, and spend much of their time regretting the pain (sometimes even physical) and fear they have caused their loved ones. Others see anger as a basically harmless vice because they do not hit anyone and their anger is short-lived, though powerful. We see in Matthew 5:21-22 that Christ put sinful anger on a par with murder.

As Christians we must put off sinful anger. When we are angry we are being foolish. This foolish behavior dishonors the Lord and it will cause great difficulty in your marriage and other relationships. God also has this to say about anger:

> Cease from anger and forsake wrath; do not fret; it leads only to evildoing.
> **Psalm 37:8**

1

> **He who is slow to anger has great understanding,**
> **but he who is quick-tempered exalts folly.**
> **Proverbs 14:29**

Definition

There are two kinds of anger mentioned in the Bible: *righteous anger* and *unrighteous anger*.

Righteous anger is indignation for holy reasons. This kind of anger is consumed with the desire for righteousness or with God's will, reputation, and honor. When God is angry, He has this kind of anger. It may be possible for Christians to have this kind of anger. Paul seemed to be righteously angry when he heard about those who were "led into sin" (2 Corinthians 11:29). Paul says in Ephesians 4:26, "Be angry and yet do not sin." This could be a reference to righteous anger or it could be a reference to the initial inclination or provocation to be angry. To be sure, righteous anger is extremely rare among men and women. Anyone who is righteously angry is not sinning, is not thinking of himself, and is in complete control. When Jesus cleared out the temple, He exemplified righteous and controlled anger (Mark 11:15-18).

> **God is a righteous judge, and a God who has**
> **indignation every day.**
> **Psalm 7:11**

Unrighteous anger takes two basic forms. One is explosive and reactionary and involves venting one's feelings (Proverbs 15:28; Ephesians 4:31). Sometimes this kind of anger is easily seen and heard and is usually called "wrath" in the Bible. The other kind of anger is more of an inward slow burn. This kind of anger is simply termed "anger" in the Bible. Both of these kinds of anger are of man and are very ungodly. Here are some typical evidences of these kinds of anger.

2

"WRATH"   "ANGER"

Vented Anger	The Slow Burn
Yelling/screaming	Clammingup/moodiness
Slamming things around	Being frustrated
Cursing	Being irritated
Telling someone off	Being disgusted
Attacking verbally/name-calling	Glaring
Hitting	Huffing/snorting

> **But now you also, put them all aside: anger, wrath, malice, slander, and abusive speech from your mouth.**
> **Colossians 3:8**

Identifying Sinful Anger

Before we can talk about changing, we need to know more about what is involved with unrighteous anger and where it comes from. Sinful anger is a deed of the flesh.

> **Now the deeds of the flesh are evident, which are: immorality, impurity, sensuality, idolatry, sorcery,** *enmities, strife, jealousy, outbursts of anger, disputes, dissensions, factions....*
> **Galatians 5:19,20** [emphasis mine]

Here are some important facts about sinful anger:

1. **Anger is natural to the fallen human heart.** It has been said, "The heart of the problem is a problem of the heart." Our hearts are desperately wicked. But for the grace of God every evil thing would come out of them. Before we can rid ourselves of anger we must admit that it is a sin problem and not blame it on a personality type, an inherited trait, or a chemical imbalance (Genesis 6:5; Jeremiah 17:9; Matthew 15:18-19 and Titus 3:3).

2. **Anger always involves thoughts and intentions.** Our hearts consist of our thoughts and our intentions or motives and more. Sinful anger begins in the mind. Because this is true,

3

anger is a willful and deliberate choice. Though the reaction of anger may be such a well-worn path that it happens very quickly, thoughts and intentions are always involved (Proverbs 4:23 and Ephesians 4:17-18).

3. **Anger is caused by not being able to attain our prideful and/ or selfish goals.** In other words, anger stems from our lusts. If you ask yourself when you are angry, "What is it I am wanting?" you will get to the root of your anger. The thing that you are wanting so badly could actually start out as a good desire, but at some point it becomes a goal or something you *must* have. Anger is an excellent tip-off that we are focused in the wrong direction. When something happens to block what we must have, we become sinfully angry (Read James 4:1-3).

4. **Anger never accomplishes God's righteous ends.** Though our anger will at times enable us to attain what we are after, it never accomplishes the righteousness of God. It never accomplishes anything worthwhile. If we are going to win the battle over anger, we must first accept the fact that when we become sinfully angry we are headed in the wrong direction. This doesn't necessarily mean that we must completely abandon a desire, but it does mean that we must do an about-face concerning our goal and how we attain it, or consider whether we even need to attain it. Read Proverbs 11:23 and James 1:20. Below is a way to picture what happens when we become sinfully angry.

5. **Anger sometimes points to something good and right that should be done about a problem instead.** Sometimes we become angry when we have a situation or a problem that we need to do something about. Sometimes we become angry because there doesn't seem to be anything else we can do. Unfortunately, when we are in this mode of thinking we are being problem-oriented rather than solution-oriented. We must discover and learn to choose God's way of dealing with problems. Even then, we must be very careful to seek the right solution for the right reasons and leave the outcome to God or we might become angry all over again. Some examples of when you need to do something right about a problem might be: when a person sins against you, when you have an over-

The Cause of Anger

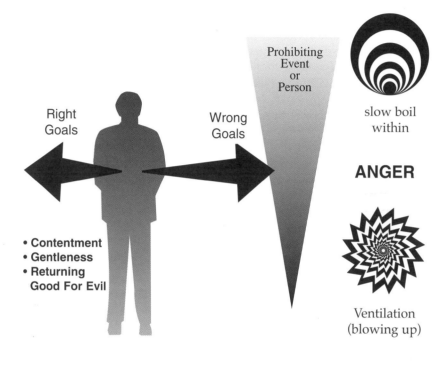

slow boil
within

ANGER

Ventilation
(blowing up)

Right
Goals

Wrong
Goals

Prohibiting
Event
or
Person

• **Contentment**
• **Gentleness**
• **Returning
  Good For Evil**

Right Goals
- Respond to problems in God's way
  or accept them as from God
- Uphold God's reputation/care
  what God thinks of me
- Serve others/help others, but leave
  them in God's hands
- Do what God wants me to do
- Pile up treasures in heaven
- Trust in God's control

Wrong Goals
**(Wicked desires or desires
turned to goals)**
- Others doing right
- No difficulty (self-focus)
- Problem removed (self-focus)
- Good treatment/respect
  (from Others) (pride)
- Personal rights observed
- Others good opinion/
  approval (pride)
- Wealth/material thing (selfishness)
- Control (self-focus/pride)
- Being better/being best
  or right (pride)
- Fulfilling a desire or plan/
  getting my way (selfishness)
- Immediate results/actions

whelming responsibility, when your schedule has been thwarted, etc. (Psalm 119:4, 9, 15, 16 and Proverbs 14:8).

6. **Anger is expressed in our thoughts, body language, speech, and actions.** Many people who struggle with anger don't see the seriousness of their problem because they may not take full action on their anger. We must remember that God sees the heart, and it is what goes on in there that makes up who we are. Even if we think we are angry only in our mind, we are still sinfully angry before God and that anger comes out in subtle but destructive ways we may not recognize. Even if it evidences itself only in a lack of communication, this is still a serious problem. In order to control our anger, we are going to have to be more aware of our thoughts, body language, and speech, not just major actions. Do not think, "It's all right if I just yell at her because I'm not physically hitting her." (Psalm 19:14 and Romans 6:12-13).

7. **Anger involves a lack of self-control.** People who struggle with anger lack self-control in their thoughts and often their deeds. They may find that they have trouble controlling themselves in other ways as well: time management, money management, lust, etc. Many times a self-control problem has been present for years. Perhaps the angry person has not controlled himself from childhood. Not controlling ourselves and merely following our initial inclinations is a choice that becomes easier and easier. While the basic problem of anger is not a lack of self-control, it will take self-control to redirect wrong thinking and learn new habits (Proverbs 17:27; 25:8; 29:11 and 2 Peter 1:6).

8. **Anger is always accompanied by other sins when it is tolerated.** We have already mentioned some of these sins. Being aware of these sins will make us more aware of anger as a true anger problem. Look for sins such as: a critical spirit, withdrawal, gossip, slander, vengeance, unwholesome words (of the mind or of speech), rejoicing in someone's misfortune, and self-pity (Proverbs 29:22).

9. **If not dealt with, anger will turn into something worse.** Anger will usually follow the progression of bitterness, stub-

bornness, hate, rebellion, and can even lead to depression and/
or suicidal tendencies (Job 4:8 and Ezekiel 18:30).

Examination

Before we discuss how to conquer anger, let us take serious
inventory of our own lives. The first step to solving a problem is
admitting that you have one. One of the worst things you can do
when you are angry is tell yourself or someone else, "I'm not
angry." Be careful of renaming anger as being "frustrated, miffed,
ticked, stressed," etc. It is also important to pinpoint specific times
and situations when you typically become sinfully angry. We all
have times when we become angry. Answer the following questions to determine when, how often, and in what manner you
become sinfully angry.

> **Search me, O God, and know my heart; try me and
> know my anxious thoughts; and see if there be
> any hurtful way in me, and lead me in the ever-
> lasting way.**
> **Psalm 139:23-24**

1. Is there anyone I am presently angry with?
2. What am I angry with them about?
3. How have I dealt with and responded to that person
   (or those persons)?
4. What do I typically do when I am angry? How might God be
   trying to reveal an anger problem to me?
5. What have been some results of my anger?
6. Do others see me as a critical or impatient person? (Ask them!)
7. When were the last five times I was angry?
8. What was my thinking at the time?
9. What kinds of things provoke me to anger?
10. Do I need to keep track in the next few weeks of when and why
    I become angry ? (When you feel irritated and frustrated, as if
    you are churning inside or ready to blow up, write down what
    you are thinking)
11. How many of these situations are precipitated by something
    else I am doing wrong? (My irresponsibility, laziness, poor
    time or money management, wrong treatment of others, etc.)

Transformation

Now that we understand anger, we can talk about what it takes to put it off and put on its righteous counterpart. Instead of anger we are to put on gentleness, patience, and humility (Ephesians 4:2, 32). Here are some things that you can do to change your angry ways:

Before anger hits again:

1. Confess your past sins of anger to God and others who have been aware of it. Explain your intentions to be gentle, patient, and humble in the future and ask for forgiveness (Matthew 5:23-24).

2. Ask God to work in this area of your life and help you to put forth full effort toward Christlike change (2 Corinthians 9:8).

3. Come up with the right thoughts to combat the wrong ones you typically have. Write them out. Use Scripture or scriptural concepts in your new thoughts. Include thankfulness in your new thoughts. Put your new thoughts in prayer form whenever you can (Romans 12:2).

Thoughts That Lead to Anger	Thoughts That Lead to Gentleness and Patience
I can't believe she is running late again! I hate being late. I insist on being on time! I'm not going to stand for this anymore!!	I don't like to be late but love is patient. I will show love to her by being patient. How can I help her to be on time more for her good? Thank you, Lord, that she takes the time to look nice.
How dare she talk to me like that! I deserve more respect than that. I will not be treated this way!	I'm not going to let my pride flare up. Lord, you didn't sin when you were not respected. What is she trying to say? I'll deal with her sin later. I'm thankful to be made aware that I have done something wrong.

Why can't the kids just do right and leave me alone! I'm tired and want to watch this TV show. They're going to get it!	Dealing with the children is my job as a parent and it pleases you, Lord. I'm tired but just give me the grace to help the children to learn. Thank you for them, Lord, and for the opportunity to teach them.

4. Memorize some verses on anger and some verses on gentleness, patience, forgiveness, or humbleness (Ephesians 4:23).

5. Since anger always involves pride, selfishness or both, seek to put on loving and humble thoughts and actions daily. Make a list of times and ways you can show love and humility (John 13:35; 1 Corinthians 13:4-7; 1 Peter 5:5).

6. Determine what godly desires and goals you should be fixed on in situations in which you typically become angry (Psalm 40:8; 1 Corinthians 10:31).

7. Do a study on the patience and long-suffering God has with you (Numbers 14:18; Psalm 145:8, 2 Timothy 2:15; *The MacArthur Topical Bible* under God's patience, longsuffering, and grace).[23]

8. Be alert, ready to exercise self-control and to change your thinking. Watch out for the situations and thoughts you have discovered. Make a concise list of each one (1 Peter 1:13).

9. Ask others to hold you accountable for your anger (Galatians 6:1-2 Hebrews 10:24-25).

10. Do not associate with angry individuals, unless they are seeking to change (Proverbs 22:24).

At the time you are tempted to become angry or are beginning to become angry:

1. Pray for God's help (Hebrews 4:16).

2. Put off being angry (Proverbs 14:17).
   - Ask yourself, "What is it I am wanting so badly?" Let go of it as something you must have. The only desire you must have is to glorify God!
   - Ask yourself, "What am I thinking that is wrong?"

3. Put on gentleness, patience, and humility (Proverbs 16:32; James 1:19).
   - Ask yourself, "What should I be thinking?" Use your new thoughts and Scripture.
   - Ask yourself, "What is the right goal?"
   - Ask yourself, "How can I be patient and think of others?"
   - Ask yourself, "What do God and others want?" and "How can I serve them?"
   - Ask yourself, "Is there something right that I should do about the problem or issue?" (Address someone's sin in the right way, plan a solution, get counsel, etc.)

If you fail and become sinfully angry:

1. Ask yourself, "How did I sin?" Be specific.
2. Ask yourself, "If I had this to do over again, what should I think and do differently?"
3. Take care of your sin of anger as soon as possible (Ephesians 4:26).
4. Confess and ask forgiveness of God and anyone else who may have been aware of or the recipient of your sinful anger. Be specific about how you were sinfully angry: wrong thinking, wrong actions, lack of love, etc. (Psalm 32:5; James 5:16).
5. Tell God and others what you plan to do in the future instead of becoming sinfully angry (Psalm 119:59-60).
6. Be on guard once again (1 Peter 5:8).

It is important that you not entertain the thinking, "This is impossible!" or "I'll never be able to change!" If you practice the principles above, you will see your anger become less and less frequent. With God's grace, God's Word, and your sincere efforts, you *will* be able to change (1 Corinthians 10:13). Remember that being tempted is not a sin, but following through with sinful anger is. Do not grow weary in "well-doing" and you will see the fruit of your efforts (Galatians 6:9). If God can change one of "the sons of thunder" (the Apostle John) into the apostle of love, He can change you (Mark 3:17; 1 John 4:7-21). A Christian who wants to exemplify Christ must be "slow to anger" and "abounding in lovingkindness."

> **The Lord is compassionate and gracious, slow to anger and abounding in lovingkindness.**
> **Psalm 103:8**

Notes

ANXIETY AND FEAR

From the time we were young children we were told, "Be brave!" "Show no fear!" This was especially true for boys. And yet we live in a society where anxiety and fear are rampant. Even though we, as Christians, should not and need not worry, we still find reasons to be anxious and fearful. Many people experience more worry than they care to admit, living in a state of anxiety and rarely having a sense of peace. Some have trouble sleeping nights and try to manage their worries and fears with medication. Still others suffer what our society labels as debilitating "panic attacks" or even worse, "nervous breakdowns."

Husbands have great potential for worry because they have such great responsibility, and wives are often overwhelmed with responsibilities of the caring for the children and upkeep of the home. We all face pressures and problems in life to one degree or another. The good news is that God speaks a great deal about anxiety and fear in His Word. He knows the difficulties we face. He has also given Christians everything they needs to trust Him and find peace of mind. The problem is that many of us don't understand anxiety and fear, or how to combat them.

Definition

Anxiety and ungodly fear are like "kissing cousins." Though they are not exactly the same, where you see one, you often see the other because they are so very closely related. Anxiety usually involves worrying about what could possibly happen. Fear goes a step further and is more convinced that what is dreaded will really happen. When someone experiences *apprehension* that does not stay within biblical bounds, there is definitely a lack of peace and trust. Concern and fear are not always wrong. Both the words *concern* and *fear* are used in the Bible to refer to right and wrong responses. There is a godly concern and an ungodly concern (anxiety). There is a godly fear and an ungodly fear.

Godly concern is caring about important things for the right reasons. It is also accompanied by a trust in God's ultimate control

13

and faithfulness. This kind of concern helps you to be responsible to God and does not send you into a confused state. It will involve a focus on *the responsibilities of today, eternal goals,* and *others*. Paul talks about the unmarried person being only "concerned" about the things of the Lord and the married person needing to be "concerned" also about pleasing his wife (1 Corinthians 7:32-33). In the New Testament reference is made to Paul's "concern for all the churches" and Timothy's "concern" for the Philippians' "welfare" (2 Corinthians 11:28; Philippians 2:20). These are examples of godly concern. For your concern to be the right kind of concern you must be focused on what is true and helpful from God's perspective.

> **So that there may be no division in the body, but that the members may have the same care for one another.**
> **1 Corinthians 12:25**

Ungodly concern (anxiety) goes beyond reasonable concern and involves worry about mere possibilities. When we are anxious, we are not focused on God and what is true and helpful. When we are anxious, we are often concerned that something *we want* to happen may not happen. Therefore, we are focused *on difficulties of the future, temporal matters,* and *self*. In Matthew 6 we are told not to worry about tomorrow and about "what we will eat," or "what we will wear for clothing" because unbelievers "eagerly seek these things" (Matthew 6:31-32). Instead, we are to concern ourselves with obeying God *today*. We are commanded not to be anxious for anything, but to trust God in everything.

> **Be *anxious* for nothing.**
> **Philippians 4:6a**

Godly fear has two parts: *the fear of God* and *reasonable fear of danger or difficulty*. When our fears fall into these two categories, we are not sinning.

- *The fear of God*: This fear is an acknowledgment of and an awe of who God is, which causes either full and glad submission to His loving will or terror of His judgment. We are all commanded to fear God (Deuteronomy 13:4). The one who loves God and delights in His will fears God as he should. This kind of fear is holy and wise and will keep us from ungodly fear.

Praise the Lord! How blessed is the man who fears the Lord, who greatly delights in His commandments. ...He will not fear evil tidings; his heart is steadfast, trusting in the Lord, his heart is upheld, he will not fear.
Psalm 112:1,7,8a

- *Reasonable fear of danger or difficulty.* There is a fear of danger and difficult circumstances that is reasonable. We would not be living in reality if we did not even consider how an upcoming situation might affect us. God wants us to live in reality, but at the same time He wants us to bring Him into the picture. It is reasonable to respond to danger and disaster. God has equipped us with a bodily response—an increase in adrenalin production—that can help us when physical danger is imminent. This increase can cause other bodily responses: pounding heart, muscle tension, heightened awareness, dry mouth, perspiration, and butterflies in the stomach. As long as we do not let our fear or our feelings keep us from doing what is right, and we turn to God in our fear, that fear is not ungodly. We are all going to feel afraid sometimes. Don't make the mistake of equating courage with a lack of feeling afraid. The most courageous Christians are those who feel afraid but place their trust in God and do what He says to do. The question is what do we do when we are afraid?

When I am afraid, I will put my trust in You.
Psalm 56:3

Ungodly fear is a certain kind of fear that we are commanded not to have (John 14:1, 27). Ungodly fear is an intimidating and often paralyzing fear. It takes many forms. Any time we cease to focus on God and others because of fear we are experiencing ungodly fear. When we do this we are focused on self. Any time we fail to do what we should do just because we are afraid of what might happen to us, we are being fearful in an ungodly way (Matthew 25:14-26; 1 Peter 3:6). We are also being fearful in a way that displeases God when we, without basis, are convinced that something dreadful will happen. Finally, when we give in to ungodly fear, we are calling God a liar (Numbers 23:19).

> **You who fear the Lord, trust in the Lord; He is their help and their shield.**
> **Psalm 115:11**

Explanation

Since anxiety always involves a certain amount of fear, for the remainder of this chapter we primarily will address fear. There are several key things we must know about ungodly fear.

1. **Ungodly fears are directly related to what we are thinking.** We have already seen that feelings come from what we think and believe. This means that what we choose to tell ourselves will either calm our fears or feed them. We must pay careful attention to our thoughts and be sure that they are "true,... honorable,... right,... pure,... lovely,... of good repute (noteworthy),... excellent,... and worthy of praise" (Proverbs 4:23 and Philippians 4:8).

2. **When sinfully fearful, we are focused on the circumstances rather than on God.** Ungodly fear and the failure to do what is right is inevitable, if we look at our circumstances without adding God and His truth into the picture. We must not only add them into the picture, but we must also dwell on them. We must fix our mind and heart on them (Genesis 32:7-12; Numbers 13:25-14:5; Psalm 55:22; Psalm 77:4-14 and Mark 4:35-41).

3. **When we are fearful we are focused on self.** Ungodly fear is selfish and therefore the opposite of love. When one continues in fear he is always focused on self and what self does or doesn't want without consideration of God and others. When we are afraid we must put on love for God and others. Love will help to dispel selfish fear (Deuteronomy 7:17-18; Isaiah 51:12-13 and Philippians 2:4).

4. **When we are engaged in ungodly fear we are fearing some-thing else more than we fear God.** This situation usually means that we want something or love something more than we want or love God. When we fear something more than God, we always forget about Him and His Word (promises) and we usually disobey Him in other ways as well. We are unfaithful to God. Read the following verses and determine what fear they were fearing more than they feared God: Job1:13-20; 3:25; Proverbs 14:26-27; 29:25; Matthew 6:31-33; 10:28; Galatians 1:10; 2:12; Hebrews 13:5-6 and 1 Peter 3:13-14.

Things we may fear more than God:	Things we may want or love more than God:
Man	Man's approval
Unwanted circumstances	Life of ease/comfort with no pain
Losing something or someone dear	Money, health, a person, things
Bodily harm	Safety, no pain

5. **Ungodly fear will most likely motivate us to commit other sins.** When we give way to ungodly fear we will be tempted to sin in other ways also. We might lie, follow the crowd, be inconsiderate of others, or even deny the Lord and His Word (Genesis 26:7; 1 Samuel 15:24; Matthew 26:69-70; and Galatians 2:12).

6. **Ungodly fear accomplishes absolutely nothing worthwhile.** Anxiety and fear have been compared to rocking in a giant rocking chair. It involves a great deal of work but doesn't get you anywhere. Worrying (sinning) never accomplishes any-thing but trouble (Proverbs 13:15; NKJV, and Matthew 6:27).

7. **Not being right with God can lead to fear and anxiety.** When a person does not know God as Savior there is often fear of death and judgement—and rightly so! Even a Christian who is

sinning usually experiences fear and anxiety about getting caught, the discipline of God, and the consequences of their sin (Psalm 38:17-18; Proverbs 14:32; Proverbs 28:1; and Hebrews 9:27).

Fear can reach paralyzing proportions when it is allowed to grow. The more a person acts on his fears instead of going against them or pushing through them, the more afraid he will become. We must be willing to endure fear if we have to in order to obey God, to be responsible, and to love others (2 Timothy 2:3-4 and 1 Peter 4:1).

Examination

Now it is time to consider your own life. The first thing you must do is admit your sins of ungodly fear and anxiety. You will have to stop calling your sin "being stressed out," "concerned," "part of my personality," or "a sickness," and certainly not talk about your worry as if it were a virtue. The second thing you must do is to put some thought into how and when you become fearful. Answer the following questions to evaluate where you are with this sin:

1. Is there anything that you are presently fearful about?
2. Recall the last 5 times you were fearful. Explain the situation that was involved. Did the situation come about due to other sins of yours?
3. What was your thinking for each of the situations in #2? Were you thinking about tomorrow? Were you concerned about temporal things or eternal things? Was your focus on unfounded possibilities? What were you fearing more than God? How were you focused: on self or not loving others?
4. How did you respond to your fear? What did you do or not do?
5. What were the results of being sinfully fearful (if you were)?
6. How were you not trusting God?
7. What have you done about those things, situations or fears since?
8. What kinds of things typically contribute to your anxiety or fear?

9. What sins do you tend to commit due to fear or anxiety? Do you lie? Do you fail to do what God wants? Are you irresponsible? Do you choose not to think of others or love others?
10. Do you need to keep track of when and why you become anxious or fearful in the next few weeks?
11. Are you sure that you are in good standing with God because you are in Christ? Are you confident that you are God's child? On what do you base your confidence?
12. Do you have any unconfessed sin in your life?

Transformation

Having come to a better understanding of ungodly fear and our own involvement with it, we can now learn exactly how to change in this area. Instead of anxiety and fear, we want to put on the fear of the Lord and trust in God's promises, love, and responsibility.

> **Be anxious for nothing, but in everything by prayer and supplication with thanksgiving let your request be made known to God. And the peace of God, which surpasses all comprehension, will guard your hearts and your minds in Christ Jesus. Finally, brethren, whatever is true, whatever is honorable, whatever is right, whatever is pure, whatever is lovely, whatever is of good repute, if there is any excellence and if anything worthy of praise, dwell on these things. The things you have learned and received and heard and seen in me, practice these things, and the God of peace will be with you.**
> **Philippians 4:6-9**

Before fear hits again:

1. Be sure that your salvation is settled and repent of any other known sin (Psalm 32:5; 1 John 5:10-13).
2. Confess and repent of your sins of ungodly fear to God and others whom your fear may have affected (Psalm 51:1-4; Matthew 5:23-24).

3. Ask God to work in this area of your life and help you to put forth full effort toward change (2 Corinthians 9:8).
4. Determine right thoughts and actions to combat the ones you usually have (see your answers above). Make your thoughts thankful, hopeful, trusting, and loving. Include Scripture in them. Try to put your new thoughts in prayer form (Psalm 119:59-60).

Fearful Thoughts	Thankful, Hopeful, Trusting and Loving Thoughts
Oh no! I just know this plane is going to crash. I can't do this. I don't want to die!	Thank you Lord, that I am in your hands. I am just as safe up here as I am on the ground. You are in control of all things. I can trust you to help me with whatever happens.
My job is ending soon and I don't have another one yet. What am I going to do? We're going to be in the poor house!	I thank you Lord, that you know our needs. I will do all I can to find another job, but I know you will help us through whatever happens. Please help me find another job. You are in control of all things. I will trust you and be content with what you provide.
If I confront his sin, he is going to get really angry, and I don't know what else he will do, but it will be really bad.	If I confront him he may be angry, but I will endure it in order to do what you want, Lord. I ask you to help him respond well, but I will trust you with whatever the outcome is.

5. Memorize some helpful verses from this chapter to help renew your mind (Romans 12:2).

6. Do a study of God's sovereignty (Isaiah 46:9-11; Genesis 50:20; Jeremiah 32:27; Romans 8:28) *
7. Do a study of God's presence and care: (Joshua 1:9; Psalm 27:1-14;Psalm 23:4). *
8. Do a study of God's sufficient grace (help) in times of trouble (Isaiah 41:10; 2 Corinthians 12:9; Hebrews 4:16).*
9. Increase your fear of God. Study, pray, and commit to love God with all your heart (Deuteronomy 10:12,20; Psalm 119:2).
10. Be alert, ready to use self-control and do battle with your thoughts (1 Peter 1:13).

During the time of fear:

1. Earnestly seek the Lord and His help (Psalm 34:4; Psalm 46:1-3).

2. Put off being sinfully fearful (Isaiah 12:2; Ephesians 4:22).
   • Ask yourself, "What am I fearing more than God?"
   • Ask yourself, "Are my thoughts headed in the wrong direction?" Are they:
     - On the future?
     - On temporal things?
     - On untrue things?
     - Focused on me?
     - Void or deficient of God and His truth?

3. Put on trust, responsibility, and love.
   • Focus most on God and His promises (Psalm 18:1-2).
   • Make yourself dwell on right thoughts and your memory verses (Ephesians 4:23).
     - Stay in the present
     - Think about eternal things and things that God is concerned with
     - Think true thoughts
     - Think profitable thoughts

   • Ask yourself, "How can I now do what is right?"
     - What is the responsible thing to do right now?
     - What is a loving thing I can do right now?
     - What constructive thing would God want me to do about this problem?

* The MacArthur Topical Bible is an excellent reference for study.

4. Be willing to endure the temptation to fear if you must in order to love God and others (2 Timothy 2:3-4).

If you fail and give way to anxiety or ungodly fear:

1. Ask yourself, "How did I sin?" Be specific about thoughts and actions.
2. Ask yourself, "If I had this to do over again, what would I think and do?"
3. Confess and ask forgiveness of God and anyone else who was affected by or who witnessed your sinful fear (James 5:16; 1 John 1:9).
4. Tell God and others what you plan to do in the future instead (Psalm 40:8).
5. Be on guard once again (1 Peter 5:8).

Fear does not have to control you. In fact, you are commanded to control fear. If you are a believer, God has given you all the resources to do this. Through practice of His principles you can conquer a pattern of anxiety or ungodly fears. If God could turn a man who denied Him three times because of fear into a courageous apostle (Peter), He can change you, too.

> **The steadfast of mind You will keep in perfect peace, because he trusts in You. Trust in the Lord forever, for in God the Lord, we have an everlasting Rock.**
> **Isaiah 26:3-4**

GOD'S PROVISIONS FOR MAN

God specifically provided for our needs. He has made a way for our salvation, our sanctification, and our glorification. If you partake of these three provisions you can become the man you were created to be.

1.   God's provision of salvation

God has provided a Savior in the person of Jesus Christ. Amazingly, He was willing to pay the penalty for the sin that *we* owe. This means that even though Jesus lived a sinless life, He, Almighty God, left heaven and the adoration He deserves in order to endure the conditions of this world, suffer shame, be rejected by men, die a criminal's gruesome death, bear the guilt of all our sins, be bitterly rejected by the Father (with whom He knew only love and harmony), and suffer the hell we so richly deserve (Philippians 2:6-8). Only Christ could do what was necessary to bring us to God.

> **For Christ also died for sins once for all, the just for the unjust, so that He might** *bring us to God*, **having been put to death in the flesh, but made alive in the spirit.**
> **1 Peter 3:18 [emphasis mine]**

It was through Christ's suffering and rejection on the cross that God's righteous wrath against sin was satisfied and a way to obtain forgiveness was made (Romans 5:9). This forgiveness is possible because God is willing to exchange Christ's righteousness for our sinfulness (2 Corinthians 5:21). For this exchange to take place a husband must have saving faith. Saving faith involves:

- Acknowledging the true reason for our existence and God's full right to our lives and how we live them (Matthew 16:24-26; Romans 11:36; 1 Corinthians 6:20).
- Coming to God in humbleness, recognizing you have nothing to offer God in your defense (James 4:6).
- Asking Him for His mercy and forgiveness, instead of what is deserved (Luke 18:9-14).

- Believing in who Christ is and His payment for your sin (1 Corinthians 15:3).
- Believing that Christ rose from the dead as Lord over all and sits at the right hand of the Father pleading the case of all those who believe (1 Corinthians 15:4; Philippians 2:9-11; Hebrews 7:25).

Christ also taught that in order to enter the kingdom of God we must be like a little child. This may smack at our manly pride but Christ was talking about important attitudes of the heart. A little child knows his place and has humble faith. A little child is dependent and needy. We must come to God with this kind of faith in order to receive His gift of salvation.

> **"Truly I say to you, whoever does not receive the kingdom of God like a child will by no means enter it at all."**
> **Mark 10:15**

If we really contemplate saving faith, we can understand why Christ said what He did to those who came to hear Him speak.

> **"Enter through the narrow gate; for the gate is wide and the way is broad that leads to destruction, and there are many who enter through it. For the gate is small and the way is narrow that leads to life, and** *there are few who find it.***"**
> **Matthew 7:13-14 [emphasis mine]**

Don't be deceived. A prayer said or a profession made in the past should not assure you of your salvation. Are you *having* saving faith *now*? Are you believing *now*? It is an ongoing (obedient and persevering) belief that demonstrates that you are a child of God. Christ offered this warning to all who would listen,

> **"Not everyone who says to Me, 'Lord, Lord,' will enter the kingdom of heaven."**
> **Matthew 7:21a**

If you have never yielded to God's plan (to be forgiven and walk with Him) I beseech you, take time right now to talk to Him about these things. Ask Him to be merciful to you, not because you deserve it, but because you know that He is the Lord God who created the universe. Confess your sins (of motive, thought, word and deed) to God and seek His forgiveness on the basis of Christ's payment for your sin. If you come to God in humility and with saving faith, He will grant you salvation.

> **[Jesus said] "All that the Father gives Me will come to Me, and the one who comes to Me I will certainly not cast out."**
> **John 6:37**

2. God's provision of sanctification

Salvation does not automatically cause us to be all that we should be. Not by a long shot! It does, however, mean that we will wholeheartedly enter into a dependent effort with God toward *change* into Christlikeness (Philippians 3:12-14; 2 Peter 3:18). We do this moment by moment because of and by the Power of the gospel. In our daily lives we must remember and apply the gospel truths. (Christ's life, Christ's death for our sin, Christ in us, Christ for us, etc.)

Sometimes we may be inclined to believe that little can be done to change our ways, but obviously this is wrong. Once we are saved, God initiates the sanctification or *growth process*. God Himself provides His Word, His Spirit, prayer, and His Church for our growth (2 Peter 1:2-11). Without these provisions we could not change in the least. On the other hand, God commands that we "exercise ourselves unto godliness" (1Timothy 4:7-9). What does this mean? The Greek word for "exercise" (*gumnazo*) is where our words gymnasium and gymnastics come from. This means that with prayer for God's help we are to put a strenuous effort into becoming more like Christ. When we do our part, we must also trust in God's work and God's promise, on the basis of what Christ did on the cross for us.

> **For I am confident of this very thing, that He who began a good work in you will perfect it until the day of Christ Jesus.**
> **Philippians 1:6**

When we do our part as a Christian, we are cooperating with God in the growth process. We do our part, first of all, by *devoting our lives to loving and living for Him, rather than self*. When a person truly comes to faith in Christ he will have a new passion—Christ.

> **And He died for all, so that they who live should
> no longer live for themselves, but for Him who
> died and rose again on their behalf.**
> **2 Corinthians 5:15**

We are to be so devoted to our Creator, that we labor to please Him with every fiber of our being. Our love for the God who created and saved us should be so great that walking with Him is more important to us than anything else in the world.

Dependently working with God in the change process also means that *we will deal with any known sin God's way*. Some people believe that God's way of dealing with sin is to simply confess it and ask forgiveness. The Bible teaches that we are to deal with our sin in a fuller and much more practical way.

When we sin, God wants us to do three things:

- Confess to God our sin and our resolve to change toward righteousness. (Proverbs 28:13; 1 John 1:9)
- Rejoice in forgiveness through Christ (Matthew 6:12).
- Ask God for His transforming grace to change. (Psalm 25:4; John 15:5).
- Repent according to God's process for change by:
  a. *Working to renew the mind with Scripture* . (Romans 12:1-2). This involves knowing Scripture about whatever sin issue is at hand well enough to *specifically* change wrong or incomplete thinking into thinking that is in agreement with God's principles and promises. We must purposefully guard and renew our minds.
  b. *Working to put off sinful actions and to put on righteous ones* (Ephesians 4:20-24). This involves putting enough thought into one's life to: (1) specifically plan how and when a particular sin will be avoided, and (2) determine specific ways to apply its righteous alternatives. True repentance does not take place without these things.

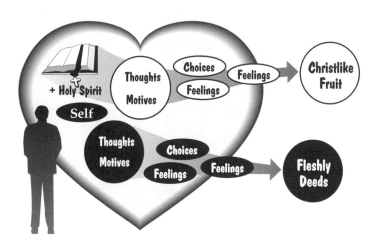

We must renew our minds because our actions flow out of our motives, thoughts and beliefs. This fact can be pictured something like this.

3. God's provision of glorification

God promises to bring us to heaven where He is and to free us from our sinful bent (1 Corinthians 15:50-58). What a great hope we have! This life is not all there is! Our short time on Earth is not what life is even about. Everything is working toward the great end of God's people being with Him for eternity (Revelation 21:3, 7).

Every Christian needs to be heavenly-minded (Colossians 3:1-3; Matthew 6:33). We will look forward to heaven more if we fully accept the fact that this life is *not* heaven, and never will be. If we live with heaven in our sights we will please God and be less likely to grow weary in the hardships of life (Hebrews 11:8-10; 12:1-3). Remembering that we will see Jesus face to face one day can also have a very purifying affect on our lives (1 John 3:2-3). We should strive to keep an eternal perspective and place *all* our hope in our future with Christ.

> **Therefore, prepare your minds for action, keep sober in spirit, fix your hope completely on the grace to be brought to you at the revelation of Jesus Christ.**
> **1 Peter 1:13**

Replacing Sinful Habits	
Sinful Thoughts, Void of God	**Thankful, Trusting, Hopeful Thoughts**
I've had it! I can't take this job anymore. (discouragement / giving up)	Lord, You know all about this difficult situation. Thank you that I have a job and that you can help me to endure. I pray that you might supply a different job if that is best. (Philippians 2:14; 4:13)
I just want to be left alone. (selfishness)	Lord, You know I don't feel like giving right now but I thank you that I have a family and that you can give me your strength. Help me to serve you and others now. (Philippians 2:3-4)
What if I lose my job? (worry)	Lord, I pray that I don't lose my job but if I do, I know that you will somehow provide. I thank you that you are faithful and in control. I trust you. (Matthew 6:25-34)

Notes

Notes

Notes